RIVER THAMES SHIPPING SINCE 2000

CARGO SHIPPING

MALCOLM BATTEN

AMBERLEY

First published 2019

Amberley Publishing
The Hill, Stroud
Gloucestershire, GL5 4EP

www.amberley-books.com

ISBN 978 1 4456 9732 1 (print)
ISBN 978 1 4456 9733 8 (ebook)

British Library Cataloguing in Publication Data.
A catalogue record for this book is available from the British Library.

Orgination by Amberley Publishing.
Printed in the UK.

Contents

Introduction

The City of London owes its existence and development to the River Thames. The site was originally chosen as a settlement by the Romans, who named it Londinium. The location was chosen as the nearest point to the estuary that the Romans could bridge the river with the technology at their disposal. The building of the first London Bridge dictated the shape of the emerging settlement. Becoming a barrier to any ships that couldn't pass under, it meant that the wharves, warehouses, docks and all other amenities associated with shipping came to be sited along the river to the east of the bridge. For several hundred years after the Romans left, London Bridge remained the only bridge in an expanding London. Other bridges would be added to the west, but it would not be until Tower Bridge opened in 1894 that a bridge was built to the east. This would remain unique until the Queen Elizabeth II Bridge opened at Dartford in 1991 – still the only bridge across the river east of Tower Bridge, and all because of the need to provide clearance for shipping.

Take a look at the River Thames in East London now and you would think that it is commercially dead. Where once the banks of the river were lined with riverside wharves, from the Upper Pool between Tower and London Bridges down to Woolwich, these have nearly all been replaced by or converted to luxury apartments. The London Docks network, including the St Katherine Docks, the East and West India Docks, the Surrey Docks on the south side of the river, and the mighty 'Royals', once the largest expanse of enclosed dockland in the world, had all closed by 1983. All have since been redeveloped as Docklands with a financial centre, London City Airport, the University of East London, houses, shopping and other amenities.

However, the commercial life of the river didn't die – it just moved downriver. But why? In the early 1960s new cargo handling technology emerged that would fundamentally affect maritime traffic. Traditionally cargo had been loaded into the holds of ships at wharves or in dock. A labour-intensive force of dockers, stevedores, crane drivers, fork-lift truck operators, etc. was needed to manipulate the cargo and ensure it was safely stowed on board in the right order for unloading. Industrial relations were poor in an industry long dominated by casual employment (as required), rather than a regular wage. Stoppages for disputes were also frequent. The advent of containers in standard sizes and needing only a crane to lift and stack them revolutionised all this. Container ships could be loaded and unloaded in hours rather than days. The Port of London Authority decided that the existing docks were not suited to such traffic and that investment to handle this new technology should be concentrated at their other port at Tilbury, 22 nautical miles downriver from London and first opened in 1886. A new container berth opened at the dock in May 1970 when an agreement on working arrangements was finally made with the dockers. In 1978 this was supplemented by a riverside container handling berth on reclaimed land at Northfleet Hope. The other major technological change was the development of roll-on/roll-off ferries, a spin-off from wartime landing craft. In fact, the world's first such vessels were former wartime LSTs, operated by the Atlantic Steam Navigation Company between Tilbury and Rotterdam from 1946 onwards. The company's first new purpose-built vessels came in 1959. The service switched to Tilbury–Antwerp in 1955, then transferred from Tilbury to Felixstowe in 1968 (they also had services between Preston and Ireland). However, other companies came to Tilbury Docks and later new terminals would be built with easy access to the M25 and Dartford Tunnel (and later bridge).

Other new investment in Tilbury saw the opening of the Grain Terminal in June 1969, the largest in Europe at the time. Some 1.3 million tons of grain are handled here each year.

The riverbanks between Woolwich and Tilbury, particularly on the north bank, were quite industrialised, with power stations, Beckton gasworks, sewage and waste treatment works, oil storage depots, etc. – the kinds of 'dirty' industries not welcomed in London. Ford also built their car factory along here at Dagenham, with its own pier. The gasworks and power stations may have gone, but many other wharves remain, including Ford's, and have now been joined by the roll-on/roll-off terminals at Purfleet, as mentioned above.

From November 2013 the new £1.5 billion DP World London Gateway container terminal at Thameshaven, on the site of the former Shellhaven oil refinery, had opened, capable of handling the largest container ships now afloat. This 1,500-acre site was developed in stages with berths and a logistics park. Now it can take three maximum size ships at a time. The existing roads and rail line to the refinery have been upgraded to provide excellent access facilities. The first service to transfer to this new terminal was the Southern Africa Europe Container Service (SAECS), which was worked by Deutsche Afrika Linien, Maersk Line, Safmarine and Mitsui OSK Lines (MOL). Other companies, such as Hamburg SUD and Hapag Lloyd, soon followed when the second berth opened in May 2014, and other services have been won since, including the G6 Alliance of six shipping lines, which replaced a service formerly using Felixstowe. This has reduced the traffic handled at Northfleet Hope, now run by Tilbury Container Services, and this now mainly handles smaller 'feeder' container ships. The Tilbury Dock itself also has some container cranes and takes container feeders, as well as having berths catering for other traffic such as forest products, steel scrap and animal feeds. The P&O ro-ro ships, plus those of FinnLines, etc., all dock here. Vehicle carriers bring in imported vehicles and take others for export and these use a berth on the river alongside the landing stage known as Tilbury Ro-Ro. Other traffics like oil and sea-dredged aggregates continue to be unloaded at various riverside wharves.

The Port of London Authority, founded in 1909 to unite the various dock companies then operating, continues to control navigation on the 95 miles of the tidal Thames from Teddington Lock to the North Sea. However, it does not now operate the Port of Tilbury – which was sold to its management in 1992 and then to Forth Ports in 1995.

The Port of London reached its peak, in terms of tonnage handled, in 1964 when a total of 61,339,000 tons passed through the port. In 2010 it was around 48,000,000 tons, but the number of ships showed a greater decline as the container ships that now predominate carry a much greater tonnage each than the old-style cargo ships.

Tilbury (along with the London Gateway) is now one of Britain's three major container ports, along with Felixstowe and Southampton. It is the main UK port for importing paper including newsprint. A 36-acre London paper terminal with 700,000 square feet of covered storage opened within the port estate in 2014. The port has fifty-six operational berths and thirty-one independent working terminals in a total estate space of over 1,000 acres. Both Tilbury and London Gateway are served by rail with regular container trains. Container throughput is currently some 16 million tons per annum. Further expansion has now been approved in February 2019 on a 152-acre site that has been acquired, formerly part of the Tilbury power station. To be known as Tilbury 2, this will comprise a roll-on, roll-off terminal and a new Construction Materials and Aggregates (CMAT) terminal, with new rail and road connections into the site.

As stated above, the old docks closed in stages. First to go were the East India Dock and Regents Canal Dock in 1967. These were operated not by the Port of London Authority but by the British Waterways Board. In 1968 the PLA closed the St Katharine Docks and London Docks. These docks, closest to London, could only handle smaller vessels and were not rail connected. The Surrey Docks, on the south side of the river, followed in 1970. These specialised in timber traffic but as more of this became shipped on pallets rather than loose, the traffic transferred to other docks. The West India and Millwall Docks closed in 1980. General cargo ceased from the Royal Docks in 1981, with scrap metal business transferring to Tilbury in 1983. After that the docks were just used for laid-up shipping until the final vessels moved out in 1985. The London Docklands Development Corporation was set up in 1981 to redevelop the West India and Millwall Docks sites and later the Royal Docks lands.

The furthest upriver that large bulk carriers now regularly venture, bringing sugar cane, is to the Tate & Lyles sugar refinery at Silvertown. Some coasters and dredgers continue further west, serving wharves towards Greenwich including Angerstein Wharf at Charlton, now the only rail connected wharf in the London area. From here trains take aggregates to various terminals around the London area. The small sand coasters of J. J. Prior continue to discharge at a terminal on Deptford Creek.

The tugs of Cory Environmental venture upriver beyond London Bridge, taking containerised rubbish from London downriver for incineration or (formerly) landfill. Other lighterage tugs or low air-draught coasters sometimes travel through central London, but the number has declined considerably since 2000.

This book takes a look at the varying commercial shipping that has worked on the Thames since 2000. A companion book will feature passenger ships, tugs, service vessels and heritage shipping. The closure of most of the upriver commercial wharves and the subsequent creation of the Thames Path has provided many viewpoints along the river. There is now a riverside path on both sides of the river from Hampton Court, via Central London, to Island Gardens, Greenwich, on the north side and the Thames Barrier on the south side, running alongside the riverbank for much of the way. The Thames Path extension continues on the north bank to the entrance of Bow Creek, while on the south side it continues from the Thames Barrier past Woolwich and Erith to Crayford Ness.

At Gravesend and Tilbury there is ready access to the riverbank and closer views are also available from Gravesend Pier. Pleasure craft run from Central London to Greenwich, and commuter ferries on to Woolwich. However, there is no regular passenger service beyond Woolwich. For many people, the only chance to photograph locations like the London Gateway from the river is on the annual season of visits by the paddle steamer *Waverley*, now owned by the Paddle Steamer Preservation Society. For around two weeks each September/October the *Waverley* operates on the Thames, running excursions to/from Tower Pier to Southend, the Thames forts, up the Medway, or on to Whitstable, Clacton or beyond. Several of the photographs in this book, including all those beyond Gravesend, have been taken on such excursions and readers are strongly recommended to patronise these tours. Not only does it make for a great day out, you will be helping to keep this grand old lady of the sea, the last seagoing paddle steamer in the world, afloat and carrying passengers. Unfortunately, the *Waverley* has had to be taken out of service and will not be working any tours in 2019 as she needs a new boiler. Details of the appeal to raise the £2.3 million funds for this and the progress in undertaking the work can be found on their website (www.waverleyexcursions.co.uk).

All photographs are by the author except where stated. Note that in a few cases background 'clutter' such as chimneys and wind turbines have been digitally removed.

Flashback

The docks in their heyday. This is a view into the West India Docks from the lock entrance on Preston's Road. Ellerman Line's *City of York*, registered in London, is in the foreground. (Photo by Reg Batten)

The container terminal at Northfleet Hope opened in 1978. An early container ship, the *Jervis Bay* (1970, 26,876 gross registered tonnage) of OCL, arrives at Tilbury in 1978. It was this ship that had initiated container services from Tilbury in May 1970. (Photo by Reg Batten)

A traffic now long gone is that of coal for the London power stations. So called 'flatirons' – colliers with a low superstructure to fit under the Thames bridges – would deliver to the upriver power stations, such as Bankside and Battersea. This is the *Tarring* (London) of Stephenson Clarke passing Tilbury in 1977. (Photo by Reg Batten)

Until 1985 domestic rubbish for landfill was not containerised but put into lighters and covered by a tarpaulin. Cory Lighterage Ltd tug *Recruit* marshalls lighters at the Gatliff Road wharf of Westminster City Council, close to Chelsea Bridge, on 10 October 1977.

Bulk Carriers/General Cargo Ships

Bulk carriers and general cargo ships regularly visit the Thames. For instance, cane sugar is delivered to the Tate & Lyle refinery at Silvertown. This has been in operation since 1878 when it was built by Henry Tate to refine cane sugar. It is not as busy now as it once was, but still receives around forty ships a year. Located just east of the Thames Barrier, this is as far upriver as large cargo vessels now regularly venture. Grain comes to the Tilbury Grain Terminal and may also be taken on from there by smaller craft. Animal feeds are imported at Tilbury Docks and steel scrap is exported. Tilbury power station, now closed and demolished, formerly received regular supplies of fuel. Aggregates from Norway come in self-unloading vessels to the docks or to riverside wharves at Northfleet.

The Tate & Lyle sugar refinery at Silvertown. On 29 February 2004 *M. Trader* is discharging at the wharf and typifies the ships that call here. In the foreground are moored tugs *Warrior* and *Aicirtron* of the Thames & Medway Towage Co. Unfortunately on this occasion a contract worker who had been using a mini bulldozer in the hold to push the raw sugar into place for the grab crane lost his life when the bulldozer became detached while being lifted out of the hold, crashed down on to the deck and then rolled overboard into the Thames.

In the first decade of the new century, some cargo ships with traditional style derricks were still visiting the river. One of the last of these I saw at Tate & Lyles was the *Stefanis* [Kingston] on 24 April 2009. Note that new grab cranes have been installed on the wharf since the 2004 picture. These were installed in October 2007 at a cost of some £3 million each.

Two days later, having discharged her cargo, the *Stefanis* passes Gravesend on her way back out to sea. Ships tend to take from two to five days to unload, depending on size.

The well-maintained German-owned fleet of Helsing & Grimm were regular visitors until their demise. The *Fione* passes Gravesend on her way upriver, probably to Silvertown, on 24 October 2006.

On 26 September 2018 the *TSL Rosemary* [Hong Kong] (2012, 21,483 grt) departs from Woolwich after discharging her cargo. Kotug tug *SD Seal*, which has assisted her, will follow her back to Tilbury. Photographed from Woolwich Arsenal Pier.

In 2003 Polish Steamship Co. (Polsteam) bulk carrier *Odra* [Nassau], bound for Tate & Lyles, was impounded on arrival after the captain was lost at sea during the voyage. She was seen in the lock entrance to King George V Dock on 26 October 2003.

Some sixteen years later and another vessel of the Polish Steamship Co., the *Olza* [Monrovia] (2012, 13,579 grt), visits Tate & Lyles in May 2019. The quayside grab crane can be clearly seen. Polsteam seems a rather dated name – it must be many years since any of their ships were steam powered!

Bulk carrier *Bahia* passing Gravesend on her way downriver on 28 June 2006. This was another ship with the earlier style of derricks, no longer to be seen on the river.

The *Federal Yamaska* [Valletta] (2013, 24,177 grt) has unloaded at the Tilbury Grain Terminal and sets sail (so to speak) on 29 March 2019. Another bulker can be seen in the background on Tower Wharf. Svitzer tug *Svitzer Cecilia* [Grimsby] has pulled her off the terminal.

On an earlier occasion in 2014, *Rochester Castle* [Valletta] (1997, 27,552 grt) is berthed on Seacon's Tower Wharf.

On 23 May 2019 *Star Hyperion* [Panama] (1996, 26,449 grt) arrives at Gravesend and will enter Tilbury Docks to load. *Svitzer Bootle* has manoeuvred into position as the bow tug, with another Svitzer tug at the stern to take her through the lock and into the dock.

Some years earlier, on 23 September 2003, the Gearbulk Shipowning Ltd *Alouette Arrow* [Bergen] is arriving at Tilbury.

On 29 August 2011 bulk carrier *Tundra* [Limassol] (2009, 19,814 grt) is outward bound passing Gravesend.

Built in Japan in 2009 and fitted with both cranes and a derrick, *Patriot SW* [Panama] departs on 8 March 2012. The pilot launch is alongside.

In 2005, Tilbury B power station was still in use and coal fired. The appropriately named *Bulk Two* [Majuro] has just berthed and is being held in place by tugs until she is fully tied up. The jetty was enlarged in 2004 and could handle ships up to 70,000 tons deadweight. Up to 2 million tons of coal a year would be unloaded here.

The *Lopi Z* [Majuro] (1997, 37,457 grt) is being unloaded at the power station on 2 October 2008. The cranes here used an Archimedean screw system to continually discharge the coal rather than the hopper grabs seen at Tate & Lyles.

A general view of Tilbury power station. The vessel being unloaded is the *Stefania Lembo* [Napoli] on 30 August 2010. New in 2010, this weighed in at 82,117 tons deadweight.

From May 2011, work began to convert Tilbury B power station to run on biomass wood pellets. However, on 27 February 2012 a major fire broke out in a fuel storage area of the station. Following this, in 2013 the owners RWE npower announced that they were ceasing conversion work. The power station was decommissioned and has since been demolished. On 12 March 2013 the *Botnia* is on the stage being unloaded.

On Tilbury Grain Terminal *BBC Russia* [Limassol] displays her offset mounted cranes. The date is 29 September 2005. The owners were Briese Schiffahrts GmbH. Grain is normally discharged by suction cranes – like a giant vacuum cleaner.

In 2019 Tilbury Docks was still receiving visits around once a month from the vessels of Westfal-Larsen from Norway, with their distinctive straddle gantry cranes. On an earlier occasion, in September 2011, the vessel arriving is the *Optimana* [Singapore] (2003, 38,910 grt).

Regular visitors to Tilbury are the self-unloading bulkers of Aboitiz Jebsen Bulk Transport trading as Mibau-Stema. These bring aggregates from Jelsa in Norway. This is *Bulknes* [St Johns] (2009, 33,171 tons deadweight) arriving on 23 May 2009.

Another of the Mibau-Stema self-unloading bulkers, *Sandnes* [St Johns] (2004, 28,000 tons), demonstrates how the boom is used to discharge her cargo of aggregates at Red Lion Wharf, Northfleet.

Another of the fleet, the *Fitnes* [St Johns], seen discharging at Red Lion Wharf in May 2019.

Cement Carrier

Dedicated cement carrier *Cembay* [Limassol] (1998) arrives at Gravesend on 27 October 2017. A Kotug tug is in attendance.

Coasters

Coasters are the workhorses of short sea trade to ports elsewhere in Britain and Europe. They come in a variety of sizes, some adapted to fit the contours of European rivers and canals with adjustable masts and superstructure for restricted clearances. They berth both within Tilbury Dock and at the many remaining riverside wharves.

A regular for many years, *Sea Shannon* [Lemmer] is owned by Seacon Group Ltd, founded in 1955 as Sea and Continental Waterways Transport Ltd. She is seen at their covered Tower Wharf at Northfleet in October 2008. This wharf is covered to allow steel imports to be unloaded in the dry in all weather conditions.

Sea Shannon sets off on another voyage in August 2018. The vessel's former name *Joriston* is visible below the current name. Built in 1998, she is 1,670 grt. One of Cobelfret's ro-ro ferries is heading round Northfleet Reach on its inward journey.

The green-hulled, Irish-owned fleet of Arklow Shipping are frequent visitors to the Thames. On 2 March 2007 one of their larger vessels, the *Arklow Wave* (Arklow, 2003), is arriving at Gravesend. She left the fleet in December 2016 and was sold to new Swiss owners.

On 27 September 2018 the *Arklow Falcon* (Arklow) is inward bound near Rainham.

On 23 October 2018 the *Arklow Rover* is loading steel scrap at Docklands Wharf, Dagenham, just east of the entrance to Barking Creek.

Other regular visitors are the Norwegian owned 'Aas' ships. Here *Aasnes* [Haugesund] is heading upriver on 2 October 2008. The twin funnel arrangement is unusual for a vessel of this type. She dated from 2001 and weighed in at 4,015 tons deadweight.

On 27 September 2018 the *Aastun* [Gibraltar] is swinging round to enter the lock at the entrance to Tilbury Docks. The grab crane mounted on a travelling gantry is a distinguishing feature of this fleet.

During the construction of Crossrail, spoil from the tunnel boring was taken by train to a terminal at Northfleet, the tracks being relaid for this purpose, and then transported by coaster to Wallasea Island, there to be used in the creation of a new wetlands nature reserve. Some 7 million tons of earth were moved. Amongst the vessels used for the purpose were some from the Norwegian HAV fleet such as *Celtica Hav* (1984), taken in August 2013.

A typical modern coaster is the *Islay Trader* [Bridgetown], seen at Gravesend. I believe this was also being used to convey Crossrail spoil at this time.

Seen from Tilbury Landing Stage, the Dutch-registered *John-Paul K* [Delfzijl] heads upriver on 27 August 2011

Dutch-owned *Maxime*, passing Greenhithe on 1 April 2013, has an adjustable bridge superstructure than can be lowered to pass under bridges on European canals.

The Belgian-owned Fast Lines are another company whose coasters can still be seen at Tilbury in 2019. Here *Fast Sus* (1996) departs in October 2009.

One company whose vessels are no longer to be seen, as they closed down in 2009, is R. Lapthorn & Co. Ltd. Their *Hoo Maple* (1989) was working within the confines of West India Dock on 28 March 2000. Along with the *Hoo Marlin* the ships were contracted to fill a cofferdam on the west side of the Heron Quays DLR station, as part of the preparations for building new offices for Deutsche Bank. They had a low enough air draught to clear the Docklands Light Railway bridge that crosses the dock.

Lapthorns *Hoofort* (1983, 1,230 tons) is approaching Imperial Wharf, Gravesend, on 17 August 2001.

Three former Lapthorns vessels, with the *Ardent* and *Swallow* nearest, are moored up at Woolwich on 18 January 2009. They were working for Coastal Bulk Services, who took over from Lapthorns.

The *River Pride* [London], formerly Lapthorn's *Hoo Pride*, heads downriver past Gravesend on 27 July 2010. The aft profile of these craft is quite distinctive.

Small coaster *Steel Sprinter* was passed near Canvey Island on 4 October 2001.

The *Windland* seen at a wharf near Greenwich in 2003.

Moored at Imperial Wharf, Gravesend, on 16 September 2003 is the *Globe,* registered at Groningen.

The *Trinity* [Bridgetown] was seen at the Erith Oil Terminal on 16 July 2005. Owned by Faversham Shipping Ltd, she dated from 1986.

Wilson Lines *Wilson Varna* is at the same location on 14 March 2019 but seen from the landward side.

Geert K has finished discharging and is backing off the Erith Oil Terminal on 7 November 2018.

Upriver Coasters

Since 1870 the small vessels of J. J. Prior have plied the Essex coast, and have been bringing sand from their quarry at Fingringhoe on the River Colne, near Wivenhoe, up to London since 1933. Here *Bert Prior* is well laden as it passes Gravesend. This was a veteran from 1961 weighing 289 tons.

Mark Prior [Colchester] (1968, 300 tons) makes the return journey, again at Gravesend in 2015. This was acquired for the fleet in 1994.

The J. J. Prior vessels are small enough to pass under the central London bridges and enable them to serve upriver discharging points. On 4 August 2005, *Francesca Prior* (1965, 261 tons) has just passed below Waterloo Bridge and is approaching Hungerford Bridge. A hatch is open, clearly showing the sand within.

Although I believe the Prior vessels no longer travel into central London to Vauxhall and Fulham, they still serve a wharf on Deptford Creek. *James Prior* (1963, 300 tons) is turning into the Creek on 25 September 2007. The towers of Canary Wharf are prominent on the other bank.

On the same day *James Prior* makes its way along Deptford Creek, with the hatches already open for unloading.

The *Polla Rose* and *Yasam Rose*, owned by J. Clubb, are among the largest upriver coasters with superstructures low enough to navigate the bridges. With a load capacity of some 700 tons, they serve various riverside wharves, including their parent Clubb Wharf, but may venture as far upriver as the Cemex (formerly RMC) wharf at Fulham. Here is *Polla Rose* at Dockland Wharf, Dagenham, in September 2018.

Another view of *Polla Rose* passing Gravesend 2 March 2010.

The *Tracy Bennett*, another vessel with a low superstructure to pass under the central London bridges, brings a cargo of sand towards Waterloo Bridge in June 2002. She was owned by Alan C. Bennett & Sons Ltd and dated from 1963.

Container Ships

The 600-metre-long Northfleet Hope container terminal can handle two medium size ships (*c.* 50,000 tons) or three of the smaller container feeders. Since 2013 it has been supplemented by the new Gateway port, which can now take three of the largest container ships afloat. Turnaround time is generally twenty-four hours for container ships or twelve hours for the smaller feeders.

Regular users of Northfleet Hope until they switched to the Gateway were Hamburg Sud. When they came to Northfleet, ships would normally berth on a Friday and sail on the Saturday. *Santa Clara* [Hamburg] (2010), *c.* 93,000 tons deadweight, is arriving at Gravesend on 29 March 2013.

The largest container ships to call at Northfleet were the 'Cap San' class of Hamburg Sud. These were just being introduced by the company when the Gateway opened, and they transferred operations there in May 2014. Only a few visits were made by the new vessels before the switch to the Gateway, and *Cap San Lorenzo* [Luxembourg], 124,479 tons, departs after the first such visit on 22 March 2014. This can carry over 9,600 TEU (i.e. 20 foot equivalent container units)

Hamburg Sud made a return to Northfleet Hope in 2018 when they once again came in on a Friday. The smaller 'Polar' class vessels are utilised on this service. *Polar Argentina* (2018, 52,156 tons dwt) was arriving on 21 June 2019. She makes an interesting comparison in size with the preserved Thames sailing barge she is passing.

One of the largest fleets of container ships is that of French company CMA CGM. They currently (2019) use both Northfleet Hope and the Gateway. On 22 March 2014 *CMA CGM Homere* [London] has just departed and passes Gravesend.

Another major fleet operator is MSC (Mediterranean Shipping Company), although they now only normally call at the Gateway. On 28 August 2010 *MSC Soraya* (2008, 73,262 tons dwt) is seen arriving from the Tilbury side of the river.

Maersk Line of Denmark are the world's largest container shipping company by both fleet size and cargo capacity. They have also now switched to the Gateway. In 2014 *Maersk Lanco* (2013, 99,900 tons dwt) is arriving. A PLA launch, the *Kew* is in the foreground.

Maersk Denia [Hamburg] arriving on 25 November 2006. Built in 2002 (45,803 tons) as the *Santa Rafaela,* this had later been the *P&O Nedlloyd Remuera*, until February 2006.

The *Dal Kalahari* [Monrovia] of Deutsche Afrika Linien in 2003. Note the twin funnels. This was built in 1978 and weighed 50,313 tons dwt.

A newer ship of the same name replaced this (2005, 63,850 tonnes) and is seen on 8 August 2006. This now sometimes calls at the Gateway.

Particularly attractive is the white livery of Safmarine from South Africa. This was the well-loaded *Safmarine Nomazwe* (2004, 63,150 tons) arriving in March 2007.

A name now passed into history is that of P&O Nedlloyd. They had been formed in 1996 as an Anglo-Dutch merger of P&O Containers Ltd (formerly OCL) and Royal Nedlloyd Lines. In 2004 Royal Nedlloyd bought the remaining shares from P&O, but then in 2005 they were acquired by the Danish A. P. Moller-Maersk Group, who merged it with their Maersk-Sealand business to form Maersk Line. The *City of Cape Town* [Southampton] (1977, 47,197 tons) departs in February 2002.

Mitsui OSK Lines *MOL Cullinan* [Hamburg] (2005, 64,519 tons) at Gravesend on 12 July 2006. Their *MOL Caledon* was the first ship on the SAECS South Africa service to berth at the new Gateway port in November 2013.

Compania Sudamericana de Vapores (CSAV) are a Chilean shipping company and the largest such company in Latin America. They were operating into Northfleet Hope in 2013. *CSAV Suape* [Monrovia] (2009, 52,726 tons) takes on tugs for berthing on 3 November.

Seen being berthed on Northfleet Hope in October 1999 is the *Contship Action* [Elsfleth] of Contship Containerlines Ltd. Tugs from Howard Smith Towage are in attendance with *Sun Surrey* on the stern. Contship was a Swiss-owned company founded in 1969 at the start of the container shipping revolution, and were taken over by CP Ships in 1997, with the name being phased out from 2006.

A 2019 view of Northfleet Hope. *CMA CGM Sambhar* [Monrovia] (2006, 51,870 tons) is the vessel on the berth on this occasion. The grain terminal can be seen in the background.

An alternative angle emphasises the size and design of the cranes that load and unload the containers. The ship in this scene from January 2017 is the *Nordserena* [Limassol], built in 2016.

At the London Gateway on 6 October 2017, one of the last few containers is being lifted from the *Alexandra* [Majuro], built in 2013.

On 27 September 2018, *MSC Bremen* [Monrovia] has completed unloading and taking on containers and is being eased off the berth by a Svitzer tug.

Mediterranean Shipping Company's *MSC Diego* [Panama] is no midget but is dwarfed by the cranes of London Gateway on 27 September 2018. The cranes were built in Shanghai, China. Each crane is 138 metres high, weighs 1,846 tons, can pick up containers twenty-five rows across deck with a maximum lifting capacity of 80 tons. They were brought over from China on board a specialist very large load carrier ship.

A year earlier and by chance it is *MSC Diego* again, heading out to sea near Southend after a visit to London Gateway.

An unusual type of container ship were the three vessels run by Seereederei Baco-Liner GmbH of Germany, trading as Baco-Liner. As well as containers these could carry twelve barges. They also had a self-unloading straddle gantry fitted. *Baco-Liner 2* [Monrovia] (1980) arrived at Gravesend on 20 September 2006.

Two months earlier, on 12 July 2006, *Baco-Liner 3* [Monrovia] was departing from Tilbury when photographed passing Gravesend. The service ended by 2010 and all three vessels were scrapped.

Container Feeders

Container feeders are the baby sisters of the container ships. They tend to serve smaller ports or pick up containers from Rotterdam, etc., on shipping routes that do not call in on London or Felixstowe.

Borchard Lines Ltd were a regular visitor in the early years of the century. *Rachel Borchard* [St Johns] approaches the end of her inward journey in September 2006. Container ship *Thuringia Express* can be seen on the Northfleet Hope berth.

Geest North Sea Line were another regular visitor. *Geest Externo* [Hamburg] (2001, 3,725 tons) departs with a symmetrical load of containers on 24 January 2004.

A regular visitor in 2013 was the Dutch-owned *Vantage* [Werkendam] (2007, 3,650 tons). Here she is approaching journey's end at Gravesend with an equally symmetrical batch of anonymous-looking containers.

In 2013 Oldenburg-Portugiesische Dampfschiffs-Rhederei (OPDR) transferred their operations from Felixstowe to Tilbury, and for a while their colourful ships could be seen heading up and down the Thames. *OPDR Lisboa* [Limassol] is arriving on 22 March 2014. Their routes served the Iberian Peninsula including the Canary Islands and North Africa, and in 2014 they were making four calls a week to Tilbury.

Typifying the feeders that visit the Thames at the time of compiling this collection in 2019 is JR Shipping's *Ensemble* [Harlingen] (2005), heading back out to sea on 27 September 2018. This is one of eighteen container feeders in this Dutch-owned fleet, along with the *Encounter, Energizer, Enforcer*, etc., which can carry 750 TEU. Larger feeders with more capacity include the *Externo, Elan* and *Elite*.

In the evening of 27 September 2018, a single crane is sufficient to service the *Grete Sibum* (2008, 13,172 tons) on Northfleet Hope.

Dredgers

A variety of dredgers, mostly British or Dutch owned, make almost daily visits to the Thames, unloading at a range of terminals on both sides of the river. They tend to dredge aggregates from designated dredging grounds either in the North Sea or off the south coast. This is a growing business, serving the building industry with aggregates for cement and concrete. A new terminal is to built as part of the Tilbury 2 project. Dredgers are also used within the docks and on the river to remove silt build-up and maintain an adequate depth at riverside wharves and in shipping lanes.

The *City of London* and *City of Westminster*, built in 1989 and 1990 respectively, were owned by United Marine Aggregates (UMA), who are now part of Tarmac. The latter is passing Erith on 25 October 2018.

Against a stormy sky, *City of Westminster* is seen again discharging at Greenhithe on 10 February 2016, with the Queen Elizabeth II Dartford bridge in the background.

Hanson Aggregates Marine Ltd dredger *Arco Humber* (1972, 8,962 tons) moored close by the Dartford bridge, which on this occasion is strangely devoid of traffic on 8 October 2000.

Hanson Group dredger *Arco Dijk* at the Greenhithe terminal in February 2015.

RMC Marine *Sand Falcon* (1998, 9,128 tons) discharges at Angerstein Wharf on 27 September 2000. This, and sister ship *Sand Fulmar*, were regular visitors to the Thames.

A similar vessel to the *City of London* and *City of Westminster* is *Britannia Beaver* of Britannia Aggregates Ltd. This was passing Gravesend on 30 July 2007.

Dutch dredger *Reimerswaal* (2012, 12,525 tons) of Reimerswaal Dredging is a regular visitor, instantly recognisable by her angled front mast (and somewhat wonky application of the name!). She was discharging at the RMC Dagenham wharf on 23 October 2018.

On the same day, the stylish *Scelveringhe* [Verseke] was discharging at the nearby De Pass Wharf. This dates from 2004.

With the same company is the similar but larger *Spauwer,* arriving at Gravesend on 6 June 2019.

Rounding the bend and approaching Gravesend pier is Dutch dredger *DC Vlaanderen 3000* (2002, 4,300 tons) in June 2017.

Passing Gravesend outward bound is the *Victor Horta* [Antwerp] on 7 May 2016.

With Tilbury power station now demolished, work has started on the Tilbury 2 project. In June 2019 dredging commenced at the former jetty. Dredger *Shoreway* has been in use at the site, the extracted material being taken to a site at South Falls for reclamation. This dredger was seen in use on 1 July.

Heavy Lift Ships

Heavy Lift ships are not regular visitors but will be brought in as required. Particular occurrences are when wharf cranes are being installed or replaced.

BigLift's *Envoyager* [Singapore] seen at Gravesend on 17 April 2006.

With the decommissioning of Tilbury power station, cranes were being removed on the *Eendracht* (2009) in 2015.

Hansa Heavy Lift *HHL Tokyo* [St Johns] swings round onto Tilbury power station to remove the final cranes on 19 February 2017.

Motor Barges

The *Gabriela*, a specialist cement-carrying motor barge, approaches Hungerford Bridge in August 2005. The poster on her side promotes the environmental advantages of transporting cement by river. She had been acquired by J. J. Prior in 2001.

Pallet Carrier Ships

The *SC Baltic* [Nassau] (1975, 3,991 tons) of SeaCargo brought wood products to Tilbury. Timber on pallets can be seen as deck cargo, with a crew member working on top of this. The two vertical structures amidships are the lift mechanism to bring cargo up from the hold. *SC Baltic* is seen here on 8 August 2006. This ship, which was also a visitor to Tate & Lyles refinery, was withdrawn and sold for scrap in 2013.

The starboard side of *SC Nordic* (1986, 4,020 tons) as it passes Gravesend in 2015. The owners are Norresundby Rederi & Shipping A/S of Norway.

While most ships that visit Tate & Lyles sugar refinery use the outer berth, the only ship that regularly used the inner berth was SeaCargo's *SC Nordic*, which called about once a month in 2018 to export refined sugar to Europe. She is seen here on 23 October 2018.

The Swedish-owned Gorthon Lines AB *Ingrid Gorthon* [Limassol] (1977) was a visitor to Tilbury in June 2007. This was possibly deputising for one of the roll-on/roll-off ships *Obbola, Ostrand* or *Ortviken* (see p. 69).

Roll-on, Roll-off

Tilbury was the first port to operate roll-on, roll-off ships when the Atlantic Steam Navigation Company started running between there and Amsterdam in 1946. They later moved to Felixstowe before becoming part of European Ferries, and since then other companies have come and gone from the Thames. The main operator since 2000 has been the Belgian company Cobelfret, who sail from Purfleet Deep Wharf, near the Dartford Queen Elizabeth II bridge to Zeebrugge and Rotterdam. They also have a contract with Ford to import vehicles from Vlissingen in Holland to the Ford jetty, and export engines from there (car production ceased at Dagenham in 2002 and now engines are made there). P&O run twice daily, most days from Tilbury Dock to Zeebrugge. Scandinavian companies use ro-ro ships to bring in forest products, etc.

Dart Line started in 1996 and operated from a terminal known as Thames Europort, close to the M25 and Dartford bridge and tunnel, on the Kent side of the river at Greenhithe. Two of their vessels including *Dart 9* [Hamilton], built in 1980 and in the foreground, are on the berth in June 2001. They had daily sailings to Zeebrugge, Vlissingen and Dunkirk.

Dart 8 [Hamilton] arriving at Gravesend shows the prominent No. 8 on the stern and the lettering promoting the service's proximity to main motorway networks. When the new Croydon trams were delivered from the makers in Vienna in 1998–99 they were transported by low-loader to Vlissingen and shipped on Dart Line ferries to Greenhithe.

Dart 3 [Nassau] (1984, 9,088 grt) passing Gravesend on 8 June 2005, outward bound with a healthy load of trailers. This was originally built as the *Balder Sten* and later became the *Bazias 3* before *Dart 3*. Note the revised funnel markings.

Dart Line were taken over by their main rivals Cobelfret in 2006. Former Dart Line *Dart 3* is seen renamed *Phocine* and with Cobelfret funnel markings while inbound at Gravesend on 21 March 2007. The launch *Recover* is used by TOSCA, an oil spill clean-up facility on the river.

Cobelfret operate from Purfleet Deep Wharf, on the north bank of the river, and again close to the M25 and Dartford bridge and tunnel. One of their older vessels, the *Eglantine* [Luxembourg] (1990, 7,225 tons) was on one of the two berths here on 4 October 2007. This was withdrawn and sold to Saudi Arabian owners in 2013.

A vessel long departed from the fleet, the *Loverval* (1978, 9,019 tons) passes Gravesend on 17 August 2001.

Cobelfret *Melusine* (1999, 9,733 tons dwt) at Ford's jetty. This is one of a batch of ships of this type built for the company in Japan in 1999–2000.

In early 2019 two of the remaining older ships, the *Cymbeline* and *Undine*, were regularly operating on the Ford service. *Undine* is seen arriving at Gravesend. The view is from the New Tavern Fort defences overlooking the river with the Fort Gardens in the foreground.

A dramatic view of another of the 1999–2000 built ferries, the *Celandine*, at Gravesend in 2018.

Although the former Dart terminal is not in regular use, it is maintained for use if required, such as if there is maintenance taking place at Purfleet Deep Wharf, or an excess of vessels. One such occasion was on 18 May 2014 when this unidentified Cobelfret vessel was on the Dart Thames Euro terminal, while others can be seen beyond the bridge at Purfleet.

One of the newer ships, the *Adeline* [Valletta] (2012), passing Gravesend en route to Ford. New imported Ford vans can be seen on deck. These will be distributed by road or rail onwards from Dagenham.

This is the *Peregrine* [Valletta] (2010, 14,538 tons dwt) at Gravesend in 2017.

Purfleet Deep Wharf at dusk. A pair of ferries load for evening sailings. In the foreground is the *Opaline*, catching the glint of the setting sun on 27 September 2018.

Ferryways started trading in 2000 and were taken over by Cobelfret in 2007. Amongst the ships acquired were the *Ipswich Way* and *Ostend Way* (reflecting one of the company's former routes). Both of these ran for a short while on the Thames with Cobelfret. *Ipswich Way* (1980, 4,538 tons) was photographed on 8 May 2008.

Another company offering roll-on/roll-off freight ferry services is P&O with a route to Zeebrugge, which started in 2007. They berth within Tilbury Dock and offer two departures most days, with one leaving *c.* 10.30 am. In 2008, the *Norcape* [Rotterdam] (1979, 6,309 tons) was one of the vessels employed and is departing past Gravesend on 17 October.

In 2019 P&O trade with the Bore.eu brand. The regular vessels in use are the *Norstream* and *Norsky*, built in 1999. The latter makes the morning departure on 29 March.

Making a once weekly journey in 2013 were the *Transpulp* and *Transtimber* of TransAtlantic, Sweden, bringing forest products as their names implied.

By 2017 these had been renamed *Thuleland* and *Tundraland* and were carrying different markings. *Thuleland* [Gothenburg] (2006, 15,960 tonnes) is entering the lock entrance to Tilbury Dock on 6 October 2017.

Transfennica of Finland also use ro-ro ships to bring in forest products on a weekly basis. *Plyca* was arriving on 1 May 2018. Other vessels on this run include *Kraftca, Pulpca, Timca* and *Trica.*

Also from Finland are Finnlines. On 8 August 2006 *Baltica* [Oslo] (1990, 13,773 tons) is passing Gravesend outward bound.

In 2019 Finnlines usually had an arrival to Tilbury Dock each Sunday morning, departing late evening. On 3 February *Finnsky* [Helsinki] (2012, 11,029 tons dwt) was the ship arriving on the service.

Another company that used to come to Tilbury on a regular basis (three times a week) was SCA Transforest. They carried forest products on wheelless cassettes, loaded by the stern doors. Three vessels were employed on this, the *Obbola, Ostrand* and *Ortviken. Obbola* [Helsingborgs] (1990, 9,589 tonnes) arrives in June 2001. The vessels saw various changes in funnel markings as they were sold by their owners, Rederi AB TransAtlantic of Sweden, to their charterers SCA Transforest in June 2011. Later the service transferred to Sheerness on the River Medway.

From July 2005, a service from Gothenberg, Sweden, was operated by DFDS Tor Line, which brought in paper for StoraEnso's new distribution centre. The return journey, in 2008, departed from Tilbury Dock on a Saturday afternoon. On 24 May *Tor Selandia* (1998, 8,700 tons) has just departed from Tilbury Dock and passes Gravesend. This was later renamed *Selandia Seaways*. This vessel was later moved to the Immingham–Cuxhaven route.

The service had become operated by Stena Line in 2009. The *Ark Forwarder* [London] (1998) was the regular vessel in use on 22 August.

Other ro-ro ships have appeared from time to time, working on hire or charter to the regular shipping lines, perhaps while vessels from their own fleet are undergoing overhaul. Cobelfret had some of their fleet working for the British Armed Forces in the early 2000s and were hiring in other ships. The *Eva Oden, Anna Oden* and *Britta Oden* of B&N were all in use, and here *Eva Oden* [Skarhahm] (1979, 16,947 tons) is seen outward bound near Canvey Island on 23 June 2001.

The *Louise Russ* [Gibraltar] was another ship that spent some time working for Cobelfret. Here it is seen in her distinctive 'ro-ro express' lettering on 20 July 2005.

This is the *Elisabeth Russ*, but this was working for Transfennica and carrying their livery when seen arriving on 27 June 2010.

Tankers

Tankers form an important part of the Thames traffic. Although the Shellhaven refinery closed and has been replaced by the London Gateway container terminal, several oil terminals receive supplies on a constant basis and there is a wide variety of ships, regular and occasional, bringing in supplies to these. Other tankers bring chemicals, bitumen, edible oils or other products.

The Vopak oil terminal is right by the Queen Elizabeth II Dartford bridge. Ships arrive here almost daily. One of the main companies is Carl Buttner GmbH. Typical of their tanker fleet is the *Seacod* [Bremen] (2006), visiting on 3 February 2019.

The setting sun glints off the river and *Hafnia Soya* [Singapore] on the evening of 27 September 2018.

Being pulled off the berth by a pair of Kotug tugs on 16 November 2013 is the *Houyoshi Express II*.

Perhaps somewhat inaptly named, a tanker called *Steel* [Majuro] departs from the Vopak terminal and prepares to negotiate the bend of St Clement's Reach in the river between Greenhithe and Tilbury. Tug *Svitzer Bootle* has been in attendance on this occasion on 6 June 2019.

A little further downriver at Grays terminal is *SW Cap Ferrat-I* on 6 October 2017.

Outward bound from Vopak or Grays is *STI Clapham* (2014, 38,736 tons) at Gravesend in 2015. This is one of a series of tankers with names of places in London including *STI Hammersmith*, *Poplar*, *Wembley*, etc., that are regular visitors to the Thames.

Also seen heading out to sea at Gravesend is the *Electa* [Bari] on 6 October 2013. *Svitzer Bootle*, which has pulled her off the berth, returns alongside the tug base at Denton, Gravesend.

Meanwhile arriving on 1 September 2008 is the *Bro Distributor* [Gothenburg], owned by Swedish company Brostrom Van Ommeren Shipping AB, whose tankers were common visitors around this time.

Another day, another tanker. An unidentified vessel arrives and is seen from the riverside at Fort Gardens, Gravesend, in June 2019.

Major storage facilities lie further downriver at Coryton, such as Oikos Storage. On 6 October 2017 the *Arsland* [Valletta] is seen here.

On 29 September 2005 *Torm Ragnhild* [Copenhagen] is arriving at Coryton and receiving the attention of a pair of tugs based there by BP, specifically for the oil tankers. The owners of this are A/S Dampskibsselskabet Torm.

Photographed near Southend on 2 October 2008 is the *Navion Torinita* [Nassau]. This will soon be leaving the area under the auspices of the Port of London Authority pilots and reaching open sea.

Moored at one of the anchorage points in the Thames estuary on 27 September 2018, while awaiting a berth, is the *Themsestern* [Douglas] owned by Rigel Schiffarts GmbH, another company whose tankers were frequent visitors. Note the prominent 'no smoking' notice.

There are other storage terminals further upriver around Purfleet and Dagenham. *Oriental Kerria* [Panama] is at one of these sites in October 2007.

A small tanker, the *Rossini*, is seen on Thunderer Jetty on 7 November 2018. This has been a frequent caller in 2018–19.

Another small tanker, the *Acacia Noir*, is viewed from Erith pier on 25 October 2018.

Imperial Wharf at Gravesend is now owned by Conways Ltd and has been adapted for the import and storage of bitumen. *Stella Virgo* [Dordrecht] is making a delivery on 23 June 2017.

A month earlier, the *Theodora* [Rotterdam] was also discharging at Imperial Wharf.

At a terminal near Purfleet in 2005 is a small chemical tanker, the *Coral Carbonic*.

This is Norsk Hydro's *Hydrogas III* [Oslo] (1975, 2,645 tons). This brought in carbon dioxide. It later became the *Yaragas III*.

LPG (liquid petroleum gas) is normally handled on the River Medway, rather than the Thames, but this tanker, the *Auteuil* [Nassau], is clearly lettered as equipped for carrying this product when seen at the Vopak terminal on 16 July 2005.

Dutch-owned tankers *Star Bonaire* [Zaandam] (1997, 3,400 tons) of Koole Tanktransport, along with the *Star Aruba* and *Star Curacao*, carry edible oils for making margarine and usually discharge at Jurgens Jetty, Purfleet. *Star Bonaire* is seen on 29 August 2011.

Tugs – Lighterage

In 1979 Cory Waste Management (now Cory Environmental) were given the contract by the Greater London Council to take containerised domestic rubbish from various loading points along the Thames to landfill sites at Rainham and Mucking. From 1985 the refuse was containerised and transported in new purpose-built barges. In 2002 they were awarded a thirty-year contract to carry waste from the Western Riverside Waste Authority – the London Boroughs of Hammersmith & Fulham, Lambeth and Wandsworth, and the Royal Borough of Kensington & Chelsea. This now goes for incineration to the Riverside Resource Recovery Facility at Belvedere, which opened in 2011. They have tugs with low superstructures to provide clearance under the central London bridges. A number of other companies employ tugs on the river, although the number is much reduced from that in the past.

Cory Environmental tug *Recruit* brings a pair of loaded lighters towards Vauxhall bridge on 11 June 2003. The chimneys of Battersea power station, once itself served by the river, can be seen in the background. This tug was originally built for Cory Tank Lighterage in 1952, but has been much rebuilt since, and is now with GPS (see p. 87).

A pair of tugs, including *General VIII*, bring lighters towards Tower Bridge, passing the preserved HMS *Belfast*, which has a visiting naval vessel on a courtesy visit moored alongside, in June 2010. *General VIII* was built in 1965 for Thames & General Lighterage Co. Ltd, who were later taken over in 1980 by Cory Lighterage Ltd. The tug was later modernised but had passed to General Marine Services by 2013.

A newer Cory tug, the *Regain*, approaching Tower bridge on 14 April 1998. This was built in Holland in 1997 as the first new tug for the Cory Environmental fleet.

Four new tugs were delivered in 2010 – the *Reclaim*, *Recovery*, *Redoubt*, and *Resource*. This is the *Recovery* approaching Tower Bridge in 2016.

One of the unloading cranes at the Riverside Resource Recovery Facility at Belvedere. The containers are placed on lorry trailers to be conveyed from the jetty into the plant.

The incineration plant in 2018. The ramped road leads to the jetty.

The main company providing tugs for towing lighters, pontoons and crane barges is GPS Marine Ltd, Chatham. This is their *Iberia* passing Gravesend in June 2012. It is in an earlier livery style and funnel markings.

In the current style is *GPS Vincia*, at Gravesend in 2013.

GPS Cervia [London] has just passed under Tower Bridge (no need to raise this) and is heading down river with a lighter in tow on 7 June 2016. This tug is the former Cory tug *Recruit* (see p. 83).

Approaching Tower Bridge with a large lighter in tow on 18 April 2019 is *GPS Cambria*. GPS have been involved in lighter traffic for the major redevelopment taking place at the former Battersea power station site.

GPS Battler is a pusher tug designed for pushing rather than towing. Here she is pulling away from the Town Pier at Gravesend after the crew had stopped there to take on provisions in town in March 2017.

Bennetts Barges tug, *Steven B* [London], has just passed under Waterloo Bridge towing a pontoon mounted crane on 20 April 2011.

Also with Bennetts Barges is *Sea Challenge II*, passing Gravesend in May 2013.

Another company making use of pusher tugs is S. Walsh & Sons. Their *SWS Norfolk* is passing Woolwich on 28 January 2019 as a plane comes in to land at London City Airport, the runway of which is located between the former King George V and Royal Victoria and Royal Albert docks.

Another S. Walsh tug is being used here to assist the paddle steamer *Waverley* in turning, after departing from Tower pier heading upriver. This will need to be turned before reaching London Bridge in order to face downriver and pass through Tower Bridge (which will be raised) at the start of another journey to Southend and beyond on 27 September 2018.

Back in 2001 many of the office blocks of the Canary Wharf financial district were still under construction. Tug *Condor IX* is assisting with bringing in materials by water through West India Dock.

Horton [Blyth] is seen positioning a lighter by the former car ferry pier at Gravesend on 4 June 2015. Built in 1968 for the Blyth Harbour Commissioners, she reached the Thames in 1979. She was acquired by the present owners J. T. Palmer & Sons of Gravesend in 2009.

From time to time, large ocean-going tugs will arrive on the Thames bringing specialist equipment from Europe for construction work, or perhaps to tow ships to or from London. On 16 October 2016, Netherlands-based tug *Dutch Blue* emerges from King George V lock having brought in an accommodation block on the pontoon, which she is returning home. She was built in 2011 and is owned by Dutch Marine Contractors.

Vehicle Carriers

A 220-metre vehicle berth with an unloading ramp, known as Tilbury Ro-Ro, is provided just to the west of the Tilbury Landing Stage. This is normally used by vehicle carriers, although some go into the dock to unload.

Eukor Car Carriers Inc. of South Korea was founded in 2002. Typical of the Eukor fleet is the *Morning Pilot* (2014), berthed at the Tilbury terminal in March 2017.

In order to align their stern ramps for unloading, vehicle carriers berth facing upriver. This means they need to be turned when departing. This stern view of the *Aniara* of Wallenius Wilhelmsen being turned clearly shows the stern loading ramp on 1 August 2018.

Not regularly seen at Tilbury are the vehicle carriers of Norwegian company Hoegh Autoliners, as these usually dock at Southampton. *Hoegh Asia* [Nassau] (2000) was a visitor on 2 June 2007.

Arriving at Tilbury on 27 February 2019 is the *Crystal Ray* [Nassau] (2000). As she slows up to await assisting tugs, she is overtaken by coaster *Maria Elise*.

On 27 September 2018, while travelling on the paddle steamer *Waverley*, we followed China Shipping's *CSCC Asia* [Nassau], which had come off Tilbury, finally catching up with her near Southend.

In 2019 there has been a weekly visit by either the *Ems Highway* or *Neckar Highway* of K Line European Sea Highway Services (KESS) in alternate weeks. On 15 May 2019, *Ems Highway* was departing. These go into Tilbury Dock rather than on the vehicle berth.

Before the regular service by *Ems Highway* and *Neckar Highway* started in 2017, KESS sent another of their ships – the larger *Danube Highway* [Nassau] – on a visit on 25 April 2017.

Vehicle Carrier/Container

Grimaldi Lines of Sicily operate a fleet of hybrid vehicle carrier and container ships, which are regular visitors to Tilbury. They go on to the vehicle berth to discharge and load vehicles, and then move on to Northfleet Hope (formerly into the dock) to offload and load their containers. *Repubblica Argentina* (Palermo) departs on 4 October 2009. The pilot launch alongside is dwarfed by the Grimaldi ship.

Grimaldi Lines *Grande Francia* [Palermo] (2002) on the vehicle berth with the tail ramp down. One of the four wind turbines now sited along the dockside can be seen. These have made photography at this location more of a challenge!

The latest ships of Grimaldi Lines are larger and carry names of places in Africa. *Grande Lagos* [Palermo] is arriving at Tilbury on 14 May 2017.

In earlier years similar format ships from Delmas Armement of France used to visit Tilbury, but no longer. *Roland Delmas* [Nassau] was departing on 14 May 2002. Delmas became a separate but wholly owned part of the CMA CGM Group, specialising in African trade routes.

Acknowledgements and Bibliography

CLAPHAM, Phoebe	*Thames Path in London* (London: Aurum, 2018)
CLEGG, W. Paul	*Docks and Ports: 2–London* (Shepperton: Ian Allan, 1987)
EVANS, Graeme	'The Tidal Thames Today' (in *Ships Monthly*, September 2004)
LUNN, Geoff	*Port of London Shipping: An Era of Change* (Stroud: Tempus, 2004)
LUNN, Geoff	*Port of London Through Time* (Stroud: Amberley, 2011)
WILTSHIRE, Andrew	*Thames Tugs in Colour* (Portishead: Bernard McCall, 2017)

Forth Ports: www.forthports.co.uk
Port of London Authority: www.pla.co.uk
Details of current shipping can be found on various websites including www.shipspotting.com